Presented To:

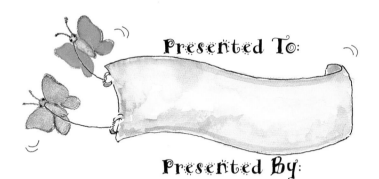

Presented By:

_____

Date:

_____

God's Little Story Book

HONOR
BOOKS

Tulsa, Oklahoma

God's Little Story Book
ISBN 1-56292-610-1
Copyright © 2000 by Honor Books
P.O. Box 55388
Tulsa, OK 74155

Written by Sarah M. Hupp
Cover and Interior Design by Whisner Design Group
Illustrated by Joanna Borero

introduction

The Bible is a storybook full of true adventures. First, it tells the wonderful story of how God created the earth. But the best stories of all are about God's people and about His Son, Jesus Christ.

So find your favorite spot, curl up with a pillow, and read about the feats of Abraham and Sarah, David and Goliath, Joseph and Mary, and Paul and Silas. Read the stories out loud with a friend. Or ask your mom or dad, grandma or grandpa, or a caregiver to read the stories to you. Learn how much God loves you and how He watches over you.

Are you ready? Then let's read!

Contents

All Things Begin

(Genesis 1:2-27)

A long, long time ago, everything was dark. There was no sun . . . no moon . . . no twinkling stars. And can you imagine a world without trees . . . or water . . . or kitty cats?

Then God said, "Let there be light!" He piled up rocks to make the mountains. He planted daisies. But best of all, he set the yellow sun up in the sky. Oh, my!

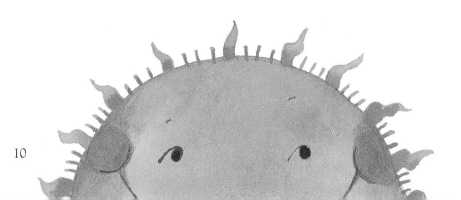

God made singing birds and swimming fish and barking dogs. Then God made the most special creation of all—people. God made Adam and Eve like Himself. And everything God made was good.

Thank You, God, for making everything good. And thank You for making me. Amen.

Adam and Eve

(Genesis 2:16—3:23)

Adam and Eve lived in a green garden called Eden. It had lots of pretty trees. God gave them bananas and nuts and berries to eat. They could eat almost every fruit . . . except one.

God told Adam and Eve not to eat the fruit of one special tree. But a mean old snake named Satan told Eve to eat it anyway. She listened to the snake and disobeyed God.

14

Eve ate the forbidden fruit. It tasted good. She shared the fruit with Adam. He ate it, too. This made God feel really, really sad. Adam and Eve had to leave the Garden of Eden.

Dear God, I don't want to make You sad.
Help me to be good.
Amen.

15

16

Noah and the Flood

(Genesis 6—8)

Noah loved God and talked to Him. One day, God told Noah to build a great, big boat. He told Noah to put two of every kind of animal on the boat . . . even skunks. Noah's family helped.

Then God shut the door. It rained . . . and rained . . . and rained for forty days and forty nights. Water covered the earth. But Noah, his family, and the animals stayed dry.

18

After many days, the boat landed on dry land. The animals were glad! Then God painted a rainbow in the sky. He promised never to make it flood like that again.

Dear God, thank You for rainbows.
Help me to listen to You just
like Noah did. Amen.

A Very Tall Tower

(Genesis 11:1-9)

Noah's children had children . . . who had children—and those children had children. And they all lived in one place. They spoke the same language. They used the same words.

The people wanted to build a tall tower. It would touch the clouds! It would reach all the way to Heaven! But they didn't ask God if it was okay.

The tower made God sad. The people loved themselves more than they loved God. So God mixed up their words. They could not understand each other. So they could not finish the tower.

Dear Lord, thank You for hearing me when I talk to You. Help me to love You more each day. Amen.

23

Abraham, Sarah, and Isaac

(Genesis 18:9-15; 21:1-7)

Abraham was an old man . . . almost a hundred years old. His wife's name was Sarah. She was old, too. They did not have any children. This made Abraham and Sarah feel sad.

But Abraham was God's friend. So God told Abraham that something special would happen. Sarah would have a baby! Sarah laughed. She said, "I am too old!"

But God said, "In one year, you will have a baby boy." And what God said came true. God never, ever lies. Sarah had a baby boy. And they named him Isaac.

Thank You, Lord, for doing what
You say You will do.
I love You! Amen.

A Rainbow Coat

(Genesis 37)

Jacob had many sons. Two of his sons were born when he was old. Jacob loved these two sons very much. Their names were Joseph and Benjamin. Joseph was a dreamer. He helped his father take care of the sheep.

Jacob gave Joseph a coat of many colors. It looked like a rainbow. It made Joseph very happy. But it made his big brothers mad. God gave Joseph a dream. Joseph told his brothers

that they would bow down to him. They
got really mad. They sold him as a slave to
Egypt. But when Joseph grew up, his dream
came true.

Thank You, Lord, for my family.
Thank You for all the nice things my
family does for me. Help me do nice
things for them, too. Amen.

33

A Boat for a Baby

(Exodus 1:20—2:10)

Many, many years passed. Jacob's sons got married. They had many babies. Pretty soon, there were as many of God's children as there were Egyptians. A bad king came into power. He wanted to kill the babies.

One mommy decided to hide her baby. She made a little boat. She put her baby in the boat. She took the boat to the river, and she hid it in the grass.

The baby began to cry. The king's daughter heard the baby and searched for him. She found the baby and said, "You can be my baby. I will call you Moses." So Moses became her son.

Thank You, Lord, for keeping Moses safe.
Thank You for keeping me safe, too.
Amen.

36

The Bush That Didn't Burn Up

(Exodus 3:1-12)

One day Moses saw a bush on fire. But the bush did not burn up. Moses went closer to look at the fire.

A voice surprised him! It was God!
God spoke to Moses out of the fire.
God said, "Take off your shoes, Moses.
This is holy ground."

God told Moses that He had a job for him to do. Moses was afraid. But God said, "Don't be afraid. I will be with you."

Dear Lord, thank You for being with me so I don't have to be afraid. Amen.

Let My People Go

(Exodus 7—12)

God's people were very sad. They were slaves. A bad king ordered his soldiers to beat them and make them work hard. But God heard their cries. God told Moses to tell the king, "Let My people go!"

41

The bad king said, "I will not let the people go." That made God angry. God allowed lots of bad things to happen to that bad king. Frogs even hopped through the palace!

But none of these terrible things touched God's people. God took care of them. And the bad king finally let the people go.

Dear Lord, help me to do what is right. And please take good care of me. Amen.

43

God Opens the Red Sea

(Exodus 13:17—14:30)

On their way home, God's people camped by the Red Sea. The bad king sent his army to kill them! The army was coming closer. But God's people could not escape. They did not have any boats.

45

God said, "Moses! Hold your stick out over the water." Moses did what God said. Then God pushed some of the water to the right. And He pushed some of the water to the left.

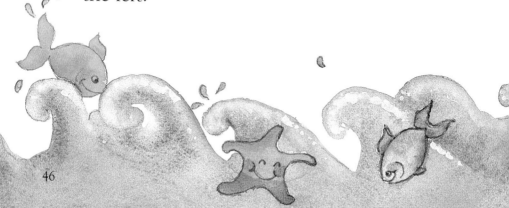

God opened a road right through the water. The people could walk through the sea on dry land. They were saved!

Thank You, God, for taking care of Your people.
Thank You for taking care of me, too.
Amen.

48

The Walls Fall Down

(Joshua 6:1-21)

The city of Jericho was proud of its strong walls. But the people of Jericho did not love God. So God said He would knock their walls down flat. God said to His people, "Walk around the city once every day."

So God's people walked around the city once every day for six days. Then God said, "Tomorrow, walk around the city seven times. On the last time around, blow the horns and shout!"

The people did what God said. They made lots of noise. And the walls fell down, just like God said they would! God gave His people the city.

Hooray for You, God!
I'm glad You are stronger than city walls.
I love You!
Amen.

David and Goliath

(1 Samuel 17:21-50)

One day, David's father told him to take food to his big brothers. They were in God's army. David was so excited! He was just a little shepherd boy. When David got to their camp, he heard a big, mean giant say bad things about God and His people.

The giant said he would kill anyone who tried to fight him. David said to the giant, "I will fight you in God's name. My God is stronger than you."

That made the giant angry! David put a small stone in his slingshot and threw it right at the giant's head. The giant fell down dead. David was a hero!

Dear Lord, help me to be brave like David. Help me to tell others how strong You are. Amen.

Three Men in the Fire

(Daniel 3)

A strong king made a bad law. He wanted people to worship him. He wanted them to bow down to his statue. If they didn't, the king would throw them into the fire. He would burn them all up!

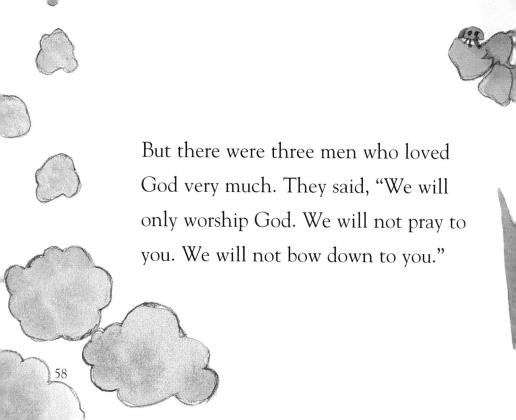

But there were three men who loved
God very much. They said, "We will
only worship God. We will not pray to
you. We will not bow down to you."

58

The king was so angry that he threw them into a hot fire. But God's angel was in the fire with them. The king was afraid! He shouted, "Come out now!" God had kept the men safe.

Dear God, help me to remember the three men. Help me to pray and love You more each day.
Amen.

60

Daniel and the Lions

(Daniel 6)

Another law said that people who prayed to God would be put in the lions' den. Daniel loved God and prayed three times a day. When some bad men saw him praying, they reported it to the king. The king liked Daniel. But he still put Daniel in the lions' den.

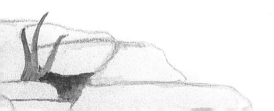

The king did not sleep all night. The next morning, he ran to the cave. He asked if Daniel was still alive. Daniel said, "I am not hurt!"

God had sent an angel to shut the lions' mouths.
The king was happy. Daniel was happy, too. God had
kept him safe.

*Dear Lord, thank You for keeping
me safe—wherever I am.
Amen.*

Jonah and the Big Fish

(Jonah 1—4)

God told Jonah to go tell some evil people about God. But Jonah didn't want to go. So Jonah ran away on a boat. But God knew where Jonah was. God knows everything!

A big storm came up. The others on
the boat found out Jonah was running
from God. So they threw him into the water.
Then a big fish ate him. Poor Jonah!

Now Jonah felt really bad that he had disobeyed. He told God he was sorry. So God gave the fish a tummy ache. And the fish spit Jonah up on dry land. Then Jonah did what God wanted.

*Dear God, I'm glad You know
where I am, too.
Help me to do what You
want me to do.
Amen.*

A Baby is Born

(Luke 1:26-35; 2:1-7)

An angel came to Mary. The angel said, "You will have a baby. Name Him Jesus." Mary told the angel that she was not married to Joseph yet. The angel said, "Your baby will be God's Son."

69

Soon it was almost time to have the baby. But Mary and Joseph had to travel to Bethlehem. The innkeeper had no room. They had to stay in the barn.

So Mary had her baby in the barn and laid Him in the hay. She named God's Son, Jesus.

Dear Lord, I'm glad that the animals shared the barn and their hay with Jesus. Help me to share my things with others, too. Amen.

Jesus Grows Up

(Luke 2:42-49)

When Jesus was twelve years old, He went to Jerusalem with His parents for the Passover. When Mary and Joseph started back home with their many friends, they thought Jesus was with them. He wasn't! Mary was so worried. Where could He be?

When Mary and Joseph returned to the city, they found Jesus at the Temple. He was talking to the priests about God. He was very wise for His age. The priests were surprised!

74

Mary scolded Jesus for making her worry. But He told her that He had been doing His Father's business. Remember? He was God's Son.

Thank You, God, for my parents.
Help them to take good care of me!
Amen.

Satan Talks to Jesus

(Matthew 4:1-11)

Jesus had gone into the desert to pray. Now He was very hungry. Satan said, "Turn the stones into bread." But Jesus would not do it. Then Satan took Jesus to the top of a building. He said, "Jump down. God will keep You safe." But Jesus refused.

Then Satan took Jesus to a very tall hill. He said, "I will give You the world if You will pray to me." Jesus said, "Go away! I will only pray to God!"

78

So Satan went away. He could not make Jesus do anything wrong. Jesus always obeyed His Heavenly Father.

Thank You, Lord, for being good.
Help me to be good every day, too.
Amen.

Jesus Feeds Lots of People

(Mark 6:30-44)

One day, thousands of people came to hear Jesus tell stories about God. They sat on rocks. They sat on the grass and under trees. They liked the stories. But soon it was time for dinner. They were very hungry!

81

Jesus told His friends to feed the people. His friends said, "We can't feed them! We only have five rolls and two fish." Jesus just smiled.

Jesus prayed, "Thank You, God, for this food." He broke the rolls into pieces. Then He broke the fish into pieces. He filled baskets and baskets with food. It was a miracle! Everyone got something to eat. There was even some left over.

Thank You, God, for giving me food to eat.
Thank You that I do not have
to go hungry. Amen.

Jesus Walks on the Water

(Mark 6:45-56)

Jesus' friends were crossing the lake in a boat. The wind started blowing hard. The men rowed hard. But they were not moving. The wind was too strong. Jesus saw that they were in danger.

So Jesus went out to the boat. He walked on top of the water. His friends had never seen anyone walk on top of the water before! They were afraid. It was a miracle!

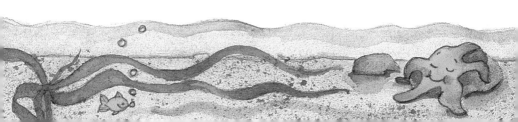

Jesus climbed into their boat. He said to the wind, "Be still!" And the wind stopped! They were able to row the boat all the way home.

Dear Lord, You helped Your friends.
I'm glad You help me when I have problems, too.
Amen.

88

Jesus Dies on the Cross

(Matthew 27:11-56)

The religious people thought Jesus was lying about knowing God. It made them angry. They did not know that Jesus really was God's Son. So they took Jesus to the ruler of the land. And some people told lies about Jesus.

Then the people yelled, "Put Jesus on a cross! Kill Him!" So the ruler did what the people wanted. He told soldiers to put Jesus on a cross.

Jesus' friends were very sad. Jesus never did anything wrong. He was good and kind. Yet Jesus died on the cross to take away our sins. Jesus loves us!

Dear God, I'm sorry that I do bad things. Thank You for letting Jesus die on the cross to take away my sin.
Amen.

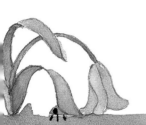

91

Jesus is Alive

(Luke 24:1-12)

After Jesus died on the cross, a friend put his body in a cave. A big rock was rolled in front of the opening. Three days later, some women wanted to see his body.

But when they got to the cave, the rock was gone. The women were so scared. Jesus' body was gone, too! And two angels sat near the cave.

The angels said, "Jesus is alive! He came back to life just like He said He would!" The women were so happy. They told everyone, "Jesus is alive!"

*Hurray, Jesus! I am glad that You
are alive again! I am glad that You
do what You say!
Amen.*

Jesus Goes Back to Heaven

(Acts 1:4-11)

It was such a great day! Jesus came back to talk to His friends. He said when He went to Heaven, God would send them the Holy Spirit to help. Jesus told them to tell everyone else about God.

97

Then Jesus floated up into the sky. A cloud came down from Heaven. It covered Jesus. When the cloud was gone, Jesus was gone.

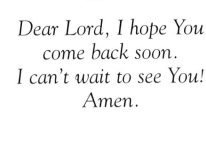

His friends kept looking for Jesus up in the sky. But they could not see Him anywhere. Two angels appeared. They said, "Jesus is in Heaven. But He will come back someday."

*Dear Lord, I hope You
come back soon.
I can't wait to see You!
Amen.*

100

Praying for Peter

(Acts 12:1-17)

Peter told many people about Jesus. But a mean king did not like it. He put Peter in jail. He put chains on Peter's hands. Poor Peter! Peter's friends prayed for him. They asked God to help.

That night, an angel came to the jail. He woke Peter up. The angel said, "Get up. Hurry!" Peter stood up, and his chains fell off. Peter was free!

The angel led Peter out of the jail. It was a miracle!

Peter's friends were so happy to see him.

Thank You, God, for helping Peter.
Thank You for helping me, too.
Thank You for hearing my prayers.
Amen.

The Ground Shakes

(Acts 16:16-40)

Paul and Silas told everyone they met about Jesus.
This made some people mad. They put Paul and Silas
in jail to stop them. They put chains on their feet.
But Paul and Silas were not sad. They sang songs.
They prayed to God.

The people in the jail heard them, too. Then the ground began to shake. The jail doors flew open. And the chains fell off their feet!

The man who took care of the jail was afraid. But Paul said, "Don't be afraid. Trust Jesus!" And the man did.

Help me, Jesus, to trust You,
too—every day and
all the time.
Amen.

107

Praise the Lamb

(Revelation 5)

Heaven is the place where God's children go when they die. It is a pretty place. The sun always shines there. Jesus lives in Heaven. He sits on a big chair called a throne. Jesus' throne is made of gold and pretty stones.

Heaven is a happy place, too.

The angels live there.

They call Jesus the Lamb.

When Jesus sits on His throne, the angels sing happy songs. They praise God. They say, "Give the Lamb praise! Give the Lamb glory!"

Wow! I want to go to Heaven, God.
I want to be Your friend.
I want to praise You forever!
Amen.

If you have enjoyed this book, or if it has
impacted your life, we would like to hear from you.
Please contact us at:

Honor Books
Department E
P.O. Box 55388
Tulsa, Oklahoma 74155

Additional copies of this book and other titles
in the *God's Little Story Book* series
are available from your local bookstore.